Hi there.

My name is Toni Kelly and I want to thank you from the bottom of my heart

for purchasing my debut poetry book and walking with me through

this written journey that is filled with lessons and lightbulbs.....

Over the years I have acquired a few life lessons of my own and forged a fair few

pearls of wisdom from my experiences. Hence the name I use on my poetry pages

 Lessons and Lightbulbs

...the lightbulb always comes after the lesson...most times anyway.

I hope you enjoy reading this book as much as I enjoyed creating it

Much love and light

T

LESSONS AND LIGHTBULBS

DEDICATION:

To my heartbeats, my children Rachel and Daniel.
Thank you for believing in me the way I believe in you.
I love you forever and a day.

LESSONS AND LIGHTBULBS

THANK YOU!

I would like to take this opportunity to say thank you!

Thank you to you, the one holding this book. Thank you to each one who has followed my poetic journey, whether it be in life, Facebook or Instagram. Your support means more than what I can even begin to describe. I am truly thankful.

To my family, those who are related by blood and to those who are related by loyalty,

I adore you

To TH and SE – I value and appreciate your encouragement and friendship.

To Jennifer Depaolis – thank you so much for taking the time to be my editor. I love you. Stay as beautiful as you are!

To my very talented daughter – thank you for the beautiful illustrations and cover

To MS Thank you for being for being my IT genius, without you this book would not have become a reality.

To LIFE – I love you and appreciate every moment you give me to enjoy, each
moment of love, sharing, caring, encouragement, art and beauty around me. I pray I never lose my love for you

LESSONS AND LIGHTBULBS

The content is as follows:

CATERPILLAR

A few sage words, mixed pieces of advice learnt and taken

with a pinch of salt

COCOON

Older pieces that helped form part of my foundation as a poet

BUTTERFLY

New pieces of my soul that are helping form an extra layer

to keep me warm in the winter months and help me fly in the summer months.

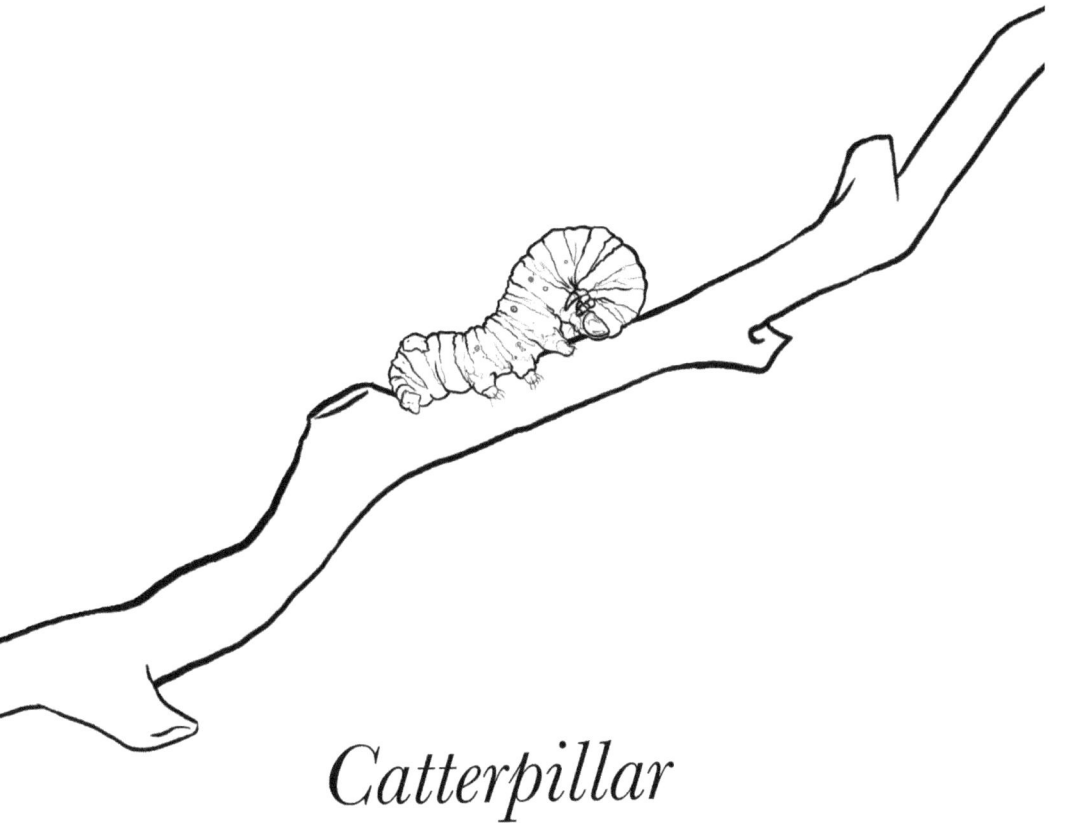

Catterpillar

LESSONS AND LIGHTBULBS

You are perfectly imperfect

> Control what you can,
> the rest ain't up
> to you

Find comfort in your own skin

> It takes more courage to be different
> than to go with the crowd

Do not be afraid of your own thoughts

> The only diet you should follow is
> balance and moderation

Live and love fully, both are a privilege

LESSONS AND LIGHTBULBS

> Questions have a yes/no answer,
> do not be offended
> when the answer is
> no

Love, loyalty, life....
three things to never take for granted

> Watch a sunset and sunrise
> at least once a week

When we clip another's
wings, they'll only want to
fly further

> Jealousy is a lack of gratitude
> I am grateful

A label is the worst
thing you can call someone

> An ego is retractable

LESSONS AND LIGHTBULBS

Regret is karmas ugly step sister
who belittles you with every chance
she can get

                                        Bravery is better than cowardice

Narrowmindedness is an
invisible, deniable disease

                                        Our sole purpose in life
                                        is to find and bring out the gold
                                        in people. People always see
                                        their flaws but forget their value

Pre-conceived ideas will most
likely always disappoint

                                          Do not use the word IF
                                        as a condition or a regret

Clichés are self-soothing
ego boosters

LESSONS AND LIGHTBULBS

> I cannot be offended by your opinion,
> your opinion is based on
>
> your character, not mine.

The word NO does not
need justification
the word YES does not
need approval

> Never assume to know
> what will do others good

Do not use the words
"I know exactly how you feel"

> Everything is based on personal
> perception.
> Do not take it personally

Blinkers are for horses not for people

> The word "promise" is for those
> who don't know how to keep their word

LESSONS AND LIGHTBULBS

Vulnerability
is strength and courage
in action

            Never tell anyone to
              "get over it"

Make sure you are loved
without masks and makeup

            Don't let other people's
             hurt and jagged pieces,
                 cut you

When your comfort zone
becomes comfortable,
move

          There's a huge difference between
            knowing and realising something

You are responsible for your own behaviour, do not expect others to be responsible for your behaviour and do not be responsible for others behaviour, it WILL lead to disappointment

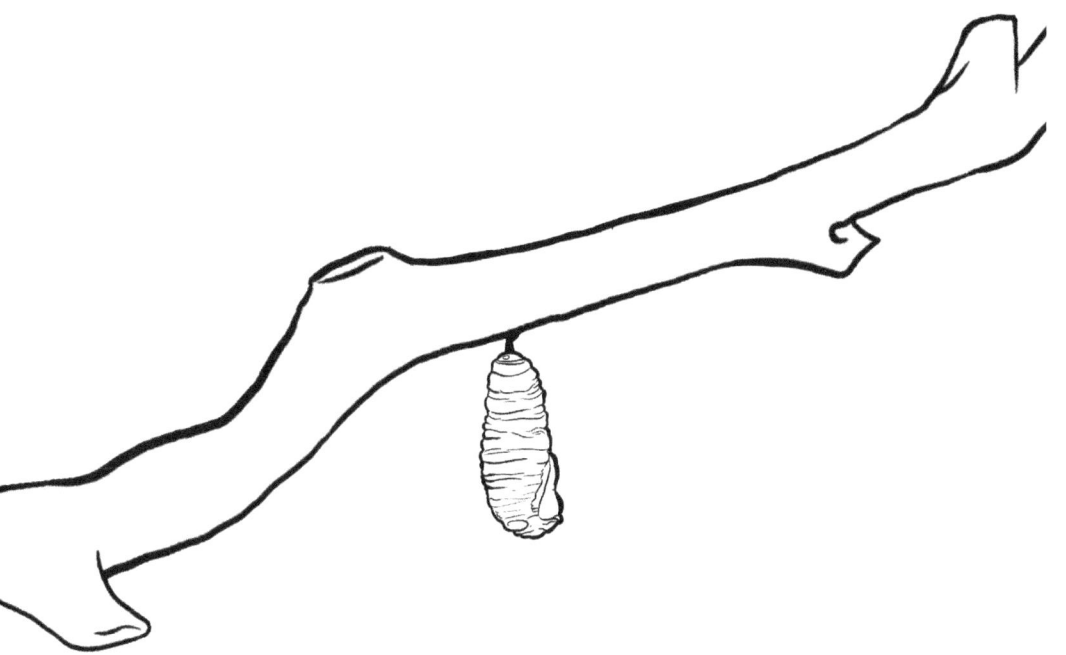

Cocoon

LESSONS AND LIGHTBULBS

IT JUST CLICKS:

One day it just clicks...

those moments where you think you couldn't survive become obsolete...

it's like a massive life light bulb

it just goes off & everything

seems so small in the greater ocean of life

like aging wine in a barrel

the hurts that scraped you

the mistakes that carved you

they just make sense and then

you wonder why the fuck

you took so long to get to where you are

and then you remember... life...

beautiful life...

that's what happened

sweet & bittersweet memories linger on

and you realise your very foundation...

the core of who you are

and always have been

has remained unchanged

those lessons & light bulbs help pave your way to the light switch...

you know the one...

the one that clicks

COURAGE:

Courage came to me once upon a day and whispered softly in my ear
Come, she said, let me take you away from here,
To a place where you'll be strong Oh no, said I, I do believe you might be wrong
Years went on and courage faded till trust had disappeared
Writing letters to another,
I had become what I had feared
my soul was torn apart by another love
Another love that had fit me like a glove
One day she came around and whispered once again
Come with me, she pleaded, let me be your strength
Oh no, said I, I'm not ready for you yet
You left me once before, you'll leave me still I bet
Then one day I finally said, "Maybe I should go ahead"
Courage heard me call that day, but my feet, they felt like lead
Never fear, she said, we'll take it day by day
I will not let you go astray
Finally, I realised that courage might be right
Maybe she could help me in my plight
Three days it took to find my feet to a strange familiar land
And all the while I felt courage hold me by the hand
Trust me, said courage once again, for now we have become like one
I was doing things I'd never dream that surely could be done
I had finally come to know that courage only grows
When that first step is taken through the dark and shady shadows
I remember her words as clear as day
She would not let me go astray So trust had turned into belief
To accomplish things, I'd never dream

COMPARTMENTS:

I don't understand how some can't do it
Especially when thoughts seem to run like fluid
Take them one by one and separate
To reveal the things, we love or hate
Thoughts and emotions should be taken apart
One for the head and one for the heart
Secrets need their own special drawer
So as to not reveal a human flaw
Filing all my thoughts away is what is best
For now I know I can get some rest
Some compartments are short and tall
Some never to reveal anything at all
Safe and sound my thoughts are to me
And I sometimes let them just run free
My secrets are mine alone
And with them I'm hard as stone
I often find I hesitate
To allow my thoughts to liberate
The need to process and to take apart
Is to me a work of art
This is who I am
It's not that I don't give a damn
It's not a mask you see
It's just who I happen to be

MUSICAL METAMORPHOSIS:

Feeling comfortable in her shell
It spun round to hold her tight
Hiding deep inside and forming wings so new
        without a conscious thought
       Time will tell if those wings can fly
       Then she hears it soft at first, a note
         that makes her stir
I know that tune, she says out loud
But her cocoon is keeping her safe
Finally, as she views her new world, she knows she's born anew
      What a great big world awaits her but she
      clings to her cocoon
      Her cocoon is still her safety net, not easy to
      let go
     Slowly as her wings begin to dry
She lifts them gently up toward the sky
Hearing it again she turns her head to listen
What is that beautiful sound she asks but it comes with no reply
         Still too close to her
     safety net
        She flaps her wings
     just once
          What freedom
     she softly cries
Oh, dear safety net, it's time to let her go
She has her new-found wings, they seem to work just fine
Letting go might not be what you want to do
        But she really is now free
      She knows that although you
     kept her safe from harm
      You are there to hear when and if she
     raises alarm
The music that she heard just set her spirit free
It was always deep within her heart, just where it ought to be....

COME CLOSER:

Inhaling deeper and deeper

I feel you nearer and nearer

Hear my heartbeat, feel my skin

Feel me from deep within

Come closer sweet lover, come listen here,

I'm calling to you with the song that only you can hear

Softly and gently you take me away

To a time and a place where we both can lay

Feeling our bodies fall and rise

Our worlds will soon collide

Come closer sweet lover, come listen here....

Pressing soft lips against mine

We try to stop the hands of time

Come closer sweet lover, come listen here,

I'm calling to you with a song that only you can hear....

LESSONS AND LIGHTBULBS

<u>DYNAMITE:</u>

Dynamite comes in small packages, so they say
But after all, who are they?
To doubt the size of a person's heart?
Who are they to throw the dart?
When looked inside you might just find
The place to where you have been assigned
To love and hold and keep us warm
From beginning of dusk to end of dawn
In small packages, you will see
The answer clear as day will be
lain old happy, truth be told
For the newly renovated and the bold
Let's not talk about a past that was
Even though it's brittle, just like glass
Fragile and broken, it is no more
For I have made it through the open door
Who are they who throw the dart
For I will not let them be a part
Of what I need to create
And the rest my dear,
is up to fate

LESSONS AND LIGHTBULBS

NO FORMAL EDUCATION:

There is no formal education for this rapid ride called life
You either become the person you thought you'd always be

or

You become the person you thought you'd never be

Sometimes there is lettered loss

of

The things you thought you knew
The things you thought were clear

Then hurt, it shook your world

and changed your point of view

MAKING PROMISES:

Making promises you just can't keep
Seriously, how is it you can lay your head to sleep
Just say what you mean and mean what you say!
Just follow through!
Enough of this
"I promise you!"
It means nothing

Nothing

Your empty words like oyster shells
with the precious gem gone missing
the precious gem of trust
just gone
Keep your promises, your empty shells
I will not live with you in that hell

LESSONS AND LIGHTBULBS

<u>TORN YOU TO SHREDS:</u>

I should've torn you to shreds

Made you

look

like my soul

like curtains clawed by cats

    good thing I know how to sew

    to mend it back together

    sewn up lines are all that remain

    in front of locked up doors

RECIPE FOR A POEM:

INGREDIENTS:

A drop of bleeding heart

A pinch of cynic soul

mix well with twisted plots

with softened edges

add a novel mind

METHOD:

Blend well to form a poem

perhaps a sonnet too I guess

whatever you feel just feel it

but add it to the recipe

there is no wrong or right

when painting pictures with our words

it is indeed after all called

a writers soul delight

LESSONS AND LIGHTBULBS

<u>IF:</u>

If.

The smallest word with the biggest effect

if you help me, I will owe you
if you hold me, I will care for you
if you hear me, I will listen to you

yes...

IF...

The loneliest word
I've heard it far too many times
so now my IF has changed to

IF

you don't like it then walk the
fuck away because you are blocking
my view

IN THE MIRROR:

The truth you seek is hiding in the mirror
and there she is
looking back at me
another wrinkle added to the collection
of my story
of my life
Who I am is written in these lines
the line of motherhood
of family
of scars

Free yourself I beg of you
Look and see the reflection
staring back at you
make sure to
grab her
hug her
love her

HOW MANLY:

How manly of you
to beat your chest....
to echo the Tarzan theme
and boldly call my name

Did you really think I'd be
impressed?

If you want to see my body
start liking me while I'm
still dressed

LESSONS AND LIGHTBULBS

<u>YOU THOUGHT:</u>

You thought
I would still be afraid
you forgot you had no hold
You thought
I'd crumble in a heap
and justify my actions
You thought
you could add another notch
upon your belt
you seem to forget the wrongs you did
and remind me all of mine.
You thought.

You
Thought.

I will not be afraid of you
I will not bow my head to you
tell all you want
about the words that are biting
at your tongue
what's done is done
you're not the only one

NO MORE GAMES:

Your heart used to be my resting place
a place where love and hate collided
I told you I want nothing more
to do with you
because you made your choice
yet you invited yourself back in and
made yourself at home
Don't dare assume I'd falter
at the mention of your name
I've had enough of all these childish games

FIRES OF THE NIGHT:

You shared with me the fire
the silent quiet one
I wished that I was there
I wished for many things that night
I knew that when I stared into
the embers of your eyes
I'd see the flame
the one that burnt your heart
I saw it broken into a million
little pieces
I wish I could have held you
I wished so hard on those fires,
The
fires
of the night

ALONE, NOT LONELY:

Being alone and lonely
are two very different things.
I don't mind one of them

ANCHOR:

If I become your anchor

we will both drown

SOBBING LULLABY:

She dropped her bag and it hit her,
gutted her like a fistless punch in the stomach
she turned to look at what was hers as tears that built up
overflowed and poured down her cheeks
she held herself in the hopes that it would soothe
her soul wept ugly tears as she dropped to her knees
on the cold hard floor
sobs of loneliness engulfed her till she could cry no more
she fell asleep with head nestled in her arm
and woke to a darkness
similar to the one that sang to her
her sobbing lullaby

THISTLE AND THORN:

Between the moss and weeds lay the things that I had dropped

Memories, they'd turned to stone

Is this really the place I once called home?

Barely unrecognisable between the thistle and the thorn

All seems lost and quite forlorn

Suddenly I see a glimpse, a shining

what had this memory garden been hiding?

I slide my hand over the moss to see

it reveals a looking glass to me,

it's a gentle reminder to never again

lose the sight of who I am

I TRIED:

I tried.
I heard you.
Didn't listen much
but hey,
I tried.

Fool me once?
Maybe I let you
but
I'm not fooled twice
You're twice the fool
for dreaming again
But I heard you.
Didn't listen much
but hey.

I tried to hear you.

I tried.

ONLY DIFFERENCE:

The only difference
between a bookstore
and a bar
is the noise

The only difference
between you and me
is the distance

The only difference
between them and us
is the moon and stars

The only difference
Between a bookstore
And a bar
Is…that you're not here

WANDERING HANDS

No one took the blame
You said it was a game
"quiet now, this didn't happen"
Wandering hands carved wounds so deep
It caused nights of eluded sleep
I guess it didn't matter when you died
I could face my fear
No longer hide

DRUNKEN CONFESSIONS:

She drank his words like sweet liqueur
Really, he seemed quite the connoisseur
Slowly sipping words of wine
She gulped each syllable sublime
Champagne bubbles rolled off his tongue
Beer belly laugh intoxicating lungs
Drunken confessions she'd heard so often
    All they did was lead to a coffin

DON'T LOSE SIGHT:

Don't lose sight of what is real

For fate and time cannot conceal

The things we truly feel

        The fate which lies before us

        We choose the path to take

        Our hopes held high

                Our dreams come true

                How far we go to make it real

                That's up to us to see it through

LESSONS AND LIGHTBULBS

SCARS IN FULL VIEW

She felt like a ship
torn apart in a storm
she used her strength as glue
as time became a sealant
She hid her scars so very well
From all the world around
then she chose a select few
to show those ragged scars to.

She didn't mind
if some people knew
because she didn't care,
she took their thoughts
with a pinch of salt
it was their point of view
she would never again
hold herself responsible
of things that people said or did
her mind was all made up
she was the only one
who could see her scars full view

CONSTANT BATTLE:

Tripping,

stumbling,

fighting

The biggest fight is with

myself

A constant battle.... what I am....

who they expect me to be

Society sees a mad man, a lover, a joker, a soldier

Fighting with myself....

push and pull

Torn between the real and mask

Twisting

Turning

pulling at hair

Hearing screams and cries at night

Just let me be! Just let me be!

What do you want?

I want to be me

Tripping,

stumbling,

fighting....

The biggest fight is with me

HAUNTING

Haunting
memories
of the man
they named
THE ONE
he'd plague your soul
till he could no more
till all had come undone
Hate, he is an ugly man
so,
if and when you see him
disobey
and run

STILL BREATHING:

In and out, yes I'm still breathing

Tap and tap, yes, my heart's still beating

Feeling? I'm not feeling much of anything.... I'm trying

I'm sad, I'm angry, I hurt

Words get stuck in my throat but wreak havoc in my mind

I'm stuck, I'm undone.... why!

Nothing makes sense

I can't believe this bullshit

Time passes way too fast

I'm trying.... I'm breathing.... it's beating....

I wish I understood....

They say get over it already

I say, bullshit!

Never.

No one knows this pain

I will keep you in my heart

In my head, in my veins

Life is forever changed

I will ride the waves till I close my eyes....

Memories are all that remain

RIOTING HEART:

I think it normal
to have a heart that fights itself

I think it's normal
to have a heart that fights a mind

Which one wins the battle of the century?
Well.
    We
        obviously can't trust
        the rioting heart

WHEN RAIN FALLS:

When rain falls and rainbow shines
Remember me, for I'm on your mind
Though shadows fall and trees they sway
Know that I am never far away

          When you whispered in my ear
          And pulled me ever near
          I felt your soul touch mine
          And I knew we were lost in time

I hear you say my name in the middle of the night
A love like ours is hard to fight
To treasure and to hold
We're not a story to be told

          God, how I miss you when you go
          But I will always always know
          That side by side we walk together
          Our hearts as one forever and ever

LOVE:

Love

isn't that loud boom you feel when you see them

Love

isn't the bell that rings when you hear them

Love

is that cheeky son of a bitch that creeps up,

slaps your ass,

pulls you closer and whispers softly

"It's called love,

you idiot"

THE TRUTH:

The truth is happiness evades those
who chose
To live in the hurt of the past
Now,
Now is all we have
Let's not squander our living rights
Let's not live in bygone fights
Open up your eyes wide
Now
is all we have

LESSONS AND LIGHTBULBS

<u>WATCH MY PULSE:</u>

I'm watching my pulse go

Tap, tap, tap

I'm still here

I'm still walking and talking

I'm still here

Were we born to only tap, tap, tap?

Do not discount me yet

I've not lost this battle

I've plenty more within

Of which I chose not to show

So, no, tap tap tap,

You may not let me go

COMFORT:

Comfort.

What a strange word.

I found comfort in your voice

Solace

in your

presence

                Comfort.

What a fucked up word indeed

LESSONS AND LIGHTBULBS

LET'S NOT TALK ABOUT THE RAIN:

Let's not talk about the rain

    Unless

    you can tell me how

    The rain conjures up

    Sweet remembrances,

    how it makes you remember

    The scent of your childhood

    ….. and catching raindrops on your tongue….

    How the rain makes you want to feel the

    Warmth of a hug

    Or a fire

Please don't just tell me about the rain

LESSONS AND LIGHTBULBS

I DON'T FORGET EASILY:

It's not that I forget easily

I simply chose to not remember

To put you in a room and slam the goddamn door

I'm not psycho because I can go from

Naught to bitch of your nightmares in

2.0 seconds

If you tear my soul

I WILL forget you

For the simple reason that you

<u>stole</u>

A piece of me

        Without my full,

        permission

LESSONS AND LIGHTBULBS

GLIDING WORDS:

You glide and hang your words
Across your lips,
Like candles waiting to be lit,
No, I will not light your path
You should not have said
Those words aloud
If words were all they were
If you did not mean a word you said
You should have kept them all unsaid

DANDELION DREAMS:

Dandelion dreams

Just blow those clean away

Dreams aren't meant to come true

for some you know

A dream

A wish

A hope

Don't dare tell me what will be, will be

What a load of bullshit

You simply couldn't see that

"the dream"

THE dream was never meant for you and me

LESSONS AND LIGHTBULBS

LOST IN WORDS:

I get lost in words

Words that bring memories to life

Words that make you remember with

A thankful heart

A grateful heart of smiles

Of days gone by

The words that make you feel the picture

with your soul

Words that bring me tears of

           Laughter

           Love

           Kindness

I get lost in all these words

TREMBLE:

Your heart trembles at the thought of feeling
        Feeling anything, so
        You reach out
        Solace is found in her embrace
        Tenderness in her kiss
                Little do you realise
                She is thinking the same
        Stepping into the unknown
        Is always a step of courage
                Like you, she doesn't want
                Her heart to break again
        So just smile and hold her
        Look, she's smiling too

LESSONS AND LIGHTBULBS

YOU ARE ENOUGH:

You are enough.

You do not need to impress

Others with falseness

You

Are

Not

Bait waiting to be caught

You are you

And you

are

enough

GHOSTS OF PAST AND PRESENT:

Inhale, said they

The ghosts of past and present

The inside of my lungs

Felt caressed with sickly smoke

Exhale slowly said *this* ghost

Let the hazy grip allow you

To choke on all your words

You've coughed up, said *that* ghost

Feel the high of once and for all

Please, inhale us

Just once more

DAGGERS IN YOUR STARE:

I can feel them you know

Through the ice of your lonely stare

Those daggers you wish to throw

Keep hurling those unsaid screams at me

I refuse to hurt you back

You can look at me in those colourful tones

I really do not mind

    All I know is simply this,

        I cannot….

      Will not

    leave you to fall behind

WOUNDED SOUL:

Wounded soul please let me see

Which bandage should I use

Where should I use it?

In the places that you hide for me to seek?

In the places that you feel might make you meek?

Kindness band aid it should be

Maybe love as ointment too

The burn of previous loves lost

Has burnt a hole where it should have not

      Tell me wounded soul,

      Which bandage should I use

LESSONS AND LIGHTBULBS

BLANK PAGE:

I turned the page to see what happens next

The morning came but forgot to bring you with it

I stared at the blank page before me

Where to and what now?

How do I write a story of our lives

If your pen has been misplaced

I thought our ink lines matched each other

In different shades of blue

I simply do not know

Where to begin

What to do

To write a story without you
                    THE END

BLEEDING POETRY:

Scribble across the lines on the blank sheet of paper

Till it all makes sense

Every ounce

Just clicks

When you lift your hand to see

All you were doing

Was simply bleeding,

bleeding poetry

LESSONS AND LIGHTBULBS

SCATTERED MOMENTS:

I tried to sweep them
Lift them all, pick them up
Scattered moments
They were sprawled on the floor
Your blue decorated hat box,
The one you gave to me… is filled with treasured memories
The hatbox, it decided to take a bow
And spill out all our treasures
Of yesteryear and now

BRUTAL TRUTH (BLACK DOG):

The brutal ugly truth is this
If you live in saddened moments
    Or in others negative worlds
    It will engulf you
    Swallow you whole
    Living in the negative starts by stealing your joy
    Gripping teeth and claws
    Will seep through every pore
    As soon as you can feel
    Its tempting touch to stay
Kick that wicked son of a bitch
    Straight back into oblivion

I AM ME:

I do not need permission
for me to be me
You also don't need that permission from me
I do not need approval
for me to just be
You also don't need that approval from me

I am me
I am what you see
Like it or not
Or leave me be

You are you
you are what I see
I'll take it or not
Or I'll leave you be

LESSONS AND LIGHTBULBS

SUN:

Sun up high in the marvellous sky

Is it not time to say goodbye

With colours bright orange red

Paint the sky colour new

Coming down so bright

Artists delight

Love pure light

Blazing

Sun

LESSONS AND LIGHTBULBS

BUSILY SERIOUS:

Yes please

No thanks

Whoop dee whoopity doo

I love a fun rhyme

You should try it sometime

Non-rhyming words are

Deliriously delicious

We don't always have to be so busily serious

LESSONS AND LIGHTBULBS

<u>REMEMBER WHO YOU ARE:</u>

Remember who you are
Before this world began raging
Their hypocrisy
Embrace the wonder that is you
Do not listen to those
Who fear their truth
Just
remember
who
you
are

LESSONS AND LIGHTBULBS

WHAT HAPPENS WHEN SILENCE HITS YOU:

When that silence hits you, it hits you damn hard.

In the gut or between the eyes, sometimes both.

You somehow find solace in words that happen to float around your mind and yet, you're happy as a lark.

You begin typing, writing, scribbling, bleeding out your soul.

The silence hits you again but this time it's gentler and you find a sense of peace at spilling your guts on paper – on screen.

You try to not let a nightmare chase you like the big bad wolf but sometimes that son of a bitch hits you to the core and you have to stop, breathe, count to 10, tell the sod to piss off and start all over again.

Days plod along and life is as you choose it but then BAM the fucking silence screams out loud again and while others think it is your heart screaming, you know it's just the quiet, your heart is way okay.

You know it's okay because it's waiting patiently.

You breathe, smile and choose happiness because that is how you prefer it.

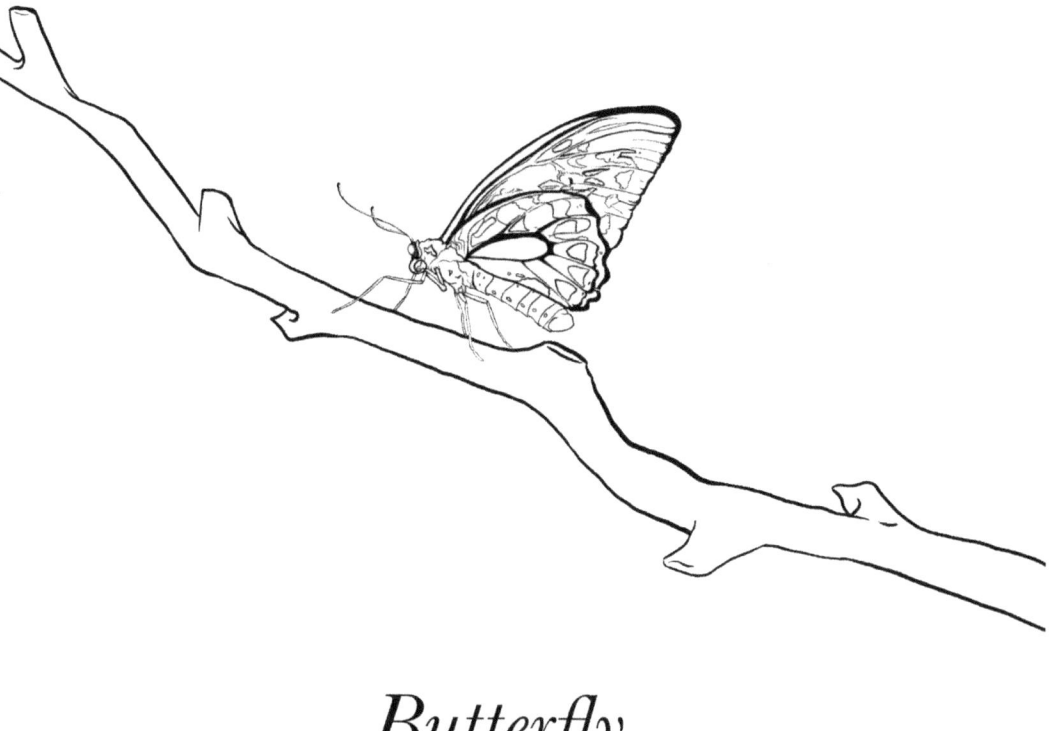

Butterfly

ABSOLUTION FROM VENGEANCE:

Sacrificing your penance more than just once
Is a poor offering
Surely, it did not cost you

A
single
damn thing

Absolution from vengeance?
Oh please!

Your guilty conscience
I will not appease

NOCTURNAL:

If you were to ask me
To choose a body part
To be nocturnal with you
I don't think I'd choose my brain….

NIGHT AIR:

Colours fade with setting sun
Moon takes shape on far horizon
Peaceful air hangs about
As stars begin to shine
Crickets start their chirping,
        It's my very favourite rhyme
        Night air fills the sky
        As I
        exhale relaxing sigh

LET'S PLAY:

She turned,

Smiled

And said

"my dark side wants to play"

CLEARING:

Create a clearing
in your head
remove the space
where fear did tread

Create a clearing
in your mind
Fear had gone
hope has been assigned

Create a clearing
In your heart
Time to walk up straight
We aren't so very far apart

DON'T LIVE THERE

Remembering the past
Is mostly beautiful
While
Living in the past
Is mostly dangerous

CHEAP PLASTERBOARD:

The walls that never did talk back
The four walls could not take the slack
She drifted
Further
Further
Further away
How much longer could she take?
Her heart was longing for much more
Than walls that were only made of
Cheap and smelly plasterboard

TWISTED:

Twisted twisted words mundane

Show me please my heart's not vain

    Feed the glory of the light

    Bathe it in effervescent sunlight

        To shine on curly twisted words

      Turn the normal, every day

    To something special, not the dreary

LESSONS AND LIGHTBULBS

HONEY PLEASE

I should tell you
But then what?
Maybe I'll find honey?
I should tell you
But then what?
It really won't be much of any benefit
But then again....
Words of slumber...
Words of rhyme...
But then again....
It really, probably, maybe, won't be of any benefit
I should tell you
But then what....?
Will I be the Queen bee?

SMALL REMINDERS

Play no part in things that do not concern you
Heed your manners
Stand up straight
Don't forget, don't be late
These things that we were taught
Were learned through children's eyes
So why? Why pray tell have the blinkers of
Those bygone days fallen by the wayside?
Yes please, do be nice
Don't let them argue with you thrice
What I need, oh Mrs please
What I need, oh Mr please
Is balance between
Kind respectful boundaries abounding
Floundering up, then down
Keeping it in a balanced state
Is easier said than done
But freedom, freedom sets you free
When you realise the power, the hold
That this has over thee

LOST

Lost in the silences of the sweet memory dream
I don't even want to scream
The walls become my pleasure
Their coldness a comforting delight
Oh, but bar the ones, who call this ragged bubble home
Sweet decadence, subservient to tasty tongue
Of cherries ripened by the senses
Just to lose it in a sweet melodic dream
Beware, she whispered in my ear
I tell you to be careful,
For from the echoed silence
Comes fearful frightened scream

TIME AND PLACE

With lips of grace and warm embrace
Their colours flowed together
His lips she traced
with fingertip
While he locked his hand
upon her hip
They braced for stormy weather

                                            This was the
                                            time and place

PUMPING HEART

I am thankful for
My pumping heart
It reminds me that
I can touch
the beautiful sound of you

AUTUMN BREEZE

Floating gracefully upon the autumn breeze
The slip of green from sturdy old oak tree
With winter around the corner
We'll wish for nights to be warmer
In awe of wondrous sunset sky
I watch the slips of brown and green pile high

MOONLIT TIME

Moonlit times it echoes most

but you don't mind the buzz of alone

the mosquitoes and spider webs will

keep you company

spilling hearts out is for brave people

and I'm not feeling very brave right now.

Just for now I'll build my bravery

till I have the courage to shout it

from the mountain tops

yes, in moonlit times

the buzz of alone

yells the loudest

PAPER PLANES

She got lost in thoughts of
Paper planes while guarding her heart
she wondered if
the guard would keep
her heart
from feeling
much of anything again
but just look....
see the
beauty of
the flying
paper
planes

IF TREES COULD TALK:

I wonder how many stories this tree could tell me....

of how seasons change its look and lustre.

Of how many secrets it **does** hold

of how the times have changed around it

yet it remained the same beautiful tree.

Just growing with the seasons

Ridding itself of old

While waiting for the new season of life.

I wish that trees could talk

because I think

we'd discover that we have a lot more in common

than we think

BLUEBERRY LIPS

I swear

I can taste you

on my tongue

your words taste

bittersweet

blueberry lips have left

my tongue wanting

more

but, sadly, my lips have turned

bright blue

CALM CHAOTIC TEARS

In the calmness of chaotic tears

My ears bleed for what they are about to hear

Who died and made you God?

Who the hell did make you judge?

You speak of "I don't see skin, wrinkles, blemishes or even beauty marks"

But what a load of hypocritical bullshit

You see it and your idle mouth spews bile

to all who care to listen to your tale of woe,

is this where you draw the line?!

The line of "once upon a wicked time

the truth I couldn't see?"

Why?

Because of your eyes.

Your filthy, painted, filtered, covered eyes

were too blind to see the blinkers

blocking your side view while you choked on others self-esteem.

Feed yourself your bullshit!

Rip the filters from your eyes,

the biggest prize is yet to come

when you see pure love through unfiltered eyes.

BONES THAT BREAK

Bones that break
then heal with time,
yet are never free of the marrows ache,
butterflies like daydreams
or words I read inside my head,
I let them flutter away
hoping they will find
a better place to land...
I have been blind and bound,
suspended inside this cerebral cocoon
for far too long,
I am beginning to find
more comfort in solitude
than in another's company
Solitude is bliss
until the bones are broken yet again
weeping marrow everywhere
butterflies return to their cocoons
it's much safer, warmer there
but life has other plans
the circle it continues
within its timely hands
our cerebral cocoon does not
like to think about
the ends of things
but only bare beginnings
thoughts drape across the midnight sky
to escape from covered cortex
via tearful sleepy eyes

FREEDOM

I begged the moon for freedom,

he said

"you have it dear"

I shouted "Freedom! Please I beg of you!"

he said

"did I not say it clear?"

I screamed so loud my lungs felt like lead

And then he said

"get it through your weary head

freedom is where angels tread..."

WORDS OF CALLOUS

Mind your words of callous

They're filled with spiteful malice

Take heed of the words that flow

Some with tarnished poisoned arrow

Mind the butterfly effect

Karma, she never tends to forget

Let the words that you do speak

Reflect a heart of truth and meek

Stones that are thrown into the water of our lives

Reverberate and multiply

Speak words of love with kindly wisdom

Altruistic ripples of simply being nice

Most of the time a kind word will indeed suffice

LESSONS AND LIGHTBULBS

THE RAVEN

The glistening raven called out to me
"Come and listen here....
Hear my words from my master and follow them real clear....
Do not waste a day on hate, remorse or deepened sorrow,
The day is there for love, not fear
Be brave and feel the heating of the sun
See it rise for you, my sweet,
Turn from east to west
The dark should be by your back
to see the glorious colour when it paints the velvet skies
Take heed, my lovely one, of the clouds that fill with rain
Remember, just like you, clouds never cry in vain
Unleash the beauty that is simply you
Let your captive self be free
Yes, sweet soul, be brave
Remember that you are made out of love
To be loved, by you, first and foremost
And no, you may not say I love me almost
So, come, come listen here, go sow the love that's deep inside
Push that fear aside
I beg you please,
don't waste a day
Days will go,
come what may

RAW

You say you like raw
But
do you really?
Live raw first and then we'll talk
Expose
those electrifying nerves
that make you feel alive
Expose
the crevices of your soul
to those who laugh and stare
those who think you haven't a hope in hell

Then…
When *that* raw is exposed
come and find me

ICE CREAM DAYS

Ice cream days
Halos fall
Horns rear their ugly heads
Testing boundaries
Living lives
Puberty our great divide
Start of adults there we go
All with hormonal glow
Joys of reaching grown up status
Is way up there
and overrated

FEEL YOUR BEATING HEART

Put your hand upon your chest
Feel your beating heart
Just by pure existence
You're beautiful as you are

Each of us is cloaked
With personalised intention
Your heart and soul should be the first
To grab a hold of their attention

SADNESS

Sadness overflows
As I lie and think of those,
The ones I love so far away
I'd love to see them another day
I've embossed them in my words
Engraved their faces with gold inside my heart
That way they will know
We'll never be apart

TO MY MOM, MY SIBLINGS, MY EXTENDED FAMILY:
I MISS YOU MORE THAN YOU REALISE

AWAKENING FRAGMENTS

Fragments of awakening
Gather round my tired soul
Wake up!
They shout in unison
Barring doubt of self
My soul it did arise
Like Sir from bended knee
Arise dear soul, the fragments say to me
Arise
And know that you are free

LOVE IS

Love
Is seeing inside your soaring soul
Smiling at the thought of you

Love
Is wondering what I can do
To make your world a better place

Love
Is acceptance, an acceptance
Of the whole: your mind, your body, your soul

Love
Is seeing every flaw
And viewing them as beautiful

Love
Is unconditional
There is no IF in love

GLASS BONES

Glass bones
Have turned to stone
Your words
No longer

      B
        R
          E
            A
              K

Me

LESSONS AND LIGHTBULBS

STRUGGLE TO SEE THE BAD

I struggle to see the 'bad' in people
We all have a drop of hell
living inside of us
the things that make us cuss and curse
my sins are no worse than yours
there is no disclaimer clause
I cannot judge your hell
My demons just won't let me.

Yes, I know…
I've taught them well

WORDS THAT FLOW LIKE WATER

I wish I had the words to say
Those words that flow like water
A dance on statued water
How seemingly our words get bolder in days
that we grow older
But this,
I use this to say
I'll find the words here after
The ones that flow like water

NOBODY FOOL

You play me
Then expect full and happy open arms?
You try to lure by using
Laughable, body boyish charm
You seem to underestimate
My crazy bitch alarm
I do not require your body
You see, I have my own
Come see me when you can think
Of something more than what
Your penis could ever hope to score
I am my own fool
But you?
You're nobody.
Fool

HALF TRUTHS

Don't take
A half truth
And make it
A full reality.
That type of poison hurts
More than one

FOUNDATION OF OUR SOULS

I guess we're all an open house
A free – for – all to view
We're liked by some,
loved by few
Often underestimated, or a renovator's dream

        Those who love us do invest
        To make themselves at home
        We'd feel quite lost without them
        They're part and parcel of who we are
        But be aware, there are a few
        Who only see the walls
        They fail hopelessly to value
        The foundation of our souls

RENAMING

Please don't insult
My intelligence
By calling me
Sexy.
…..
That
privilege
is earned

AFFIRMATION

My personal affirmation
is quite simple really:

To love, accept and forgive
myself
as I would others ….
　　　　　Unconditionally

WHY I WRITE

Why do I write?
I have to.
To me it's like breathing
Big gasp in…
Hold it…. hold it
My soul needs to exhale
But not just yet
Hold it…. hold it….
Exhale words to keep me alive
Heart beats to rhythm and rhyme
Words flow the same way gravity pushes me down
Like lyrics woven into music
I have to breathe. I have to live.
I have to write

HUMAN ABSTRACTS

Humans are abstractly beautiful

Dimension adrift galore

Some with grace

Some with sweetness

Deliciously delectable

Some totally desirable

But true abstract beauty

Will always and forever remain

The wonderful human brain

How heart and soul interact and dance

together

Is the blissful epitome

of the

human abstracts

that we are

BREATHE AND BELIEVE

I didn't believe in most of my strength

I couldn't believe till I learned how to stand

How to walk a straight line

Without holding your hand

I had no choice when they didn't see

I had no choice but the strength was within me

I had it all the time

    All you need

    If you wish to retrieve

    Is close your eyes,

        Breathe and believe

LESSONS AND LIGHTBULBS

CERTAIN MUSIC

As a certain music plays
It sways
echoes
resonates
In the deepest crevices
of my open soul a
and makes it want to

DANCE

Till morning light

LOVE AND LIGHTNING

What is the difference between
love and lightning?

Not much in some cases

THE BEAUTIFUL YOU

The truth is we're all going to have days
Days when our light doesn't shine as bright
Days when big feels small and small feels big
Days when the mirrors reflection is not what you think
Days when thoughts and feelings invade
to make you feel as ugly as sin
or as beautiful as a Queen

Days that drag or go too fast and some you wish would last
Please remember on those days
You ARE
the beautiful you
You are not what the mirror reflects
Hold fast to what defines you.
                                You.

                              The beautiful you

LAMENTING LULLABY

On my sleeve in open view
    Red satin flowed anew
        Water streamed from tired eyes
            While mind twists round most its thoughts

    Hush now baby, please don't cry
        Come, lay down, let us sing
            Lamenting Lullaby

BLEEDING HEART

Not all will understand a
Bleeding
Heart
Because
Not all
can stand
the sight
of
blood

DO WHAT MAKES YOU HAPPY

Doing what makes you happy does not make you selfish.
Doing what makes you happy,
in a world that throws various things at you
that they believe will make you happy, is called freedom.
Freedom to say

No thanks

I create my own happiness and I do that by looking in the mirror first
I have found that those who disagree aren't particularly fond of reflections.
But my God, when you find that inner happiness
Without all the bullshit, clichés and twisted tricks,
you are the happiest you will ever be.

Cling to THAT like it is your last hope
because in some cases,

It is

TELL ME

    Tell me your untruths
                not just your truths
    Tell me your disbeliefs
                not just your beliefs

    Why?

    Tell me your fear and nightmares
                not just your hopes and dreams

    Why?

    Tell me your distastes
                not just your tastes
    Tell me your sadness
                not just your happiness

    Why?

Because the latter I will find in your every day

DO NOT SPEAK OF HATRED

How dare we speak of hatred

When we cannot love ourselves

Look right in the mirror

See that person there?

Love that reflection with all its flaws

And God-forbid mistakes

Love that

And only then

Can you talk of the love of other men

TRUTH OR DARE

I love this time

The hours between 1 and 3 a.m

Drunk with soberness and tiredness

Walls are somewhat fragile

Our souls speak open truths

They say drunken mouths speak sober truth

At 3 a.m that's very true

Raw and uncut versions of ourselves

Walls are sent in for repair

And words come out for truth or dare

LESSONS AND LIGHTBULBS

LITTLE MISS TALKALOT

I like to talk a lot

sometimes

Because most times

My mouth is

closed

off

to the world

FLAME

In the depths

of the

deepest

W

A

T

E

R

I found

my brightest flame

WRINKLES

In each blessed line

A passage through time

A frown

A fear

A smile

All surrounded

by laughter lines

When joy shows up upon on your skin

you know that you are blessed within

SMILE

S earch

M y

I ntricate

L imitations, set me free with

E loquence

MIDNIGHT DAWN

Midnight black
Is the dawn of
Midnight musings

EVERYTHING YOU KNOW:

Every letter you string together

to make a new word

Every word you sew

To form a sentence

Every sentence that creates

A candid conversation

Every syllable you breathe

Every single thing you say… and don't,

Springs from everything you've ever known

MADE OF STARS

We're all made of stars

Of infinite colour

Some worlds apart

Each seek a soul and

Each seek a heart

Dancing auroras

Of life made with love

Finding our lights

That fight like a glove

LIFE REFLECTIONS

Her life reflected

Some sort of semblance

Of

"I'm really doing okay"

To

"what the hell am I doing"

So she called it a happy medium

Because that's the million dollar question

"What are we doing?"

I guess our human goals are simple

To love, to be loved

To accept, to be accepted

To want, to be wanted

Hell, if I knew all the answers

I would be writing something

Completely different

COLOURED CLICHES

If I could colour with clichés I would colour you with….

Blue for calm

Red for lust

Purple for loyal

Green for serene

And above all

Yellow for happiness

But I loathe clichés…. so I won't

PUZZLE LINES

I don't want someone to

"Hug my pieces back together"

I am not broken

I want someone to smile, trace the puzzle lines

Of where I put myself back together

And say,

"Strength,

it suits you"

POISON

The poison

I drink

I savour

At my own risk

The drink

I seek

Is only for the meek

Life is worth the chance of poison

It won't kill you, you'll savour

Each and every growing change

STATEMENT

If

you are going

to make

a statement,

Don't mumble

Say

What you need to say

Speak it

Say it

Loud and clear

Let the world

Know that

<u>You</u>

<u>Are</u>

<u>Here</u>

OVER YOU

I know I'm over you but in the blink

Of but a single

                word

Memories come seeping back

I wish to tell you lots of things….

That you echo deep

                within

I knew I had a room for you, a dark and secret one,

You were it's only key

I know you told me

                always

But always

Is almost as long as forever

LESSONS AND LIGHTBULBS

I COULD WRITE ABOUT FAIRY TALES

I could write about fairy tales…..even though they're pretty,
We all know they're just not true
I want to write about

Blood, sweat, weeping…. Survival

How you can recognise the beauty that is you
Stir in you an acceptance revival
Acceptance of

Blood, sweat, weeping…. Survival

Try to make you see that every time you open your beautiful baby
blues
It's time to fall in love with all that does surround you
If I can do all that for you with one

Verse, rhyme, poem…. word

My soul will smile forever

BETE NOIRE

Most people

are my

bete noire

…. But you're ok

FAVOURITE STRIDE

I cried so many tears for you
You never saw me
      Why?
I went into the darkened space
With tears of anger running down my face
Landslide creeping in
Ravaged soul just sickening
      But yet I rose
Goddammit did I rise!
I rose higher than you ever thought I could

So please, take your high horse for a ride
    With my favourite 'fuck you' stride

WHISKY AND WINE

Talk in shadows

Whisper hues

    Keep them rocking

    Sunshine blues

        Knock on angels door

        Leave your halo on the floor

            Bring the whisky and the wine

            Let's while away the time

LEAVE A MARK

I might not have lived a rough and tumble life
But I have lived
My scars might not look the same
But they're still scars
My hurts might not be the same
But I still hurt

Pain is pain
Whether in your head
Your heart
Your veins

Each of us get to leave a mark
Whether in a heart
A head
A vein

THE PHOENIX

You chose the phoenix to remind you
    You see it
        Every day
It's in plain and open view
Remember that she rose
    With fire in her belly
    Restored from ashes,
        Set free from broken tears
No longer to hide in her fears
Courage is her virtue
Honesty her grace
Most can see her freedom clearly
    Engraved in phoenix face

SHE LOVED HERSELF

The day she realised it didn't matter

And it never really did

That day,

That day was her turning point

What they thought of her

How they thought of her

It didn't even matter

For the very simple reason that

She had learned to love herself

TARNISHED PIECES

Pieces left along the wayside

They cannot be revived

    I stumbled across a few of them

      to get to where I am

        You cannot click your fingers and
wish that I was there

It doesn't work that way

Maybe I am cold and callous to blurt out a definite NO

      But you left me with no choice

Did you not realise that I could use my voice?

          Snip snap fingers
      all you like

           but I
           refuse to do
           more running

      You dropped pieces of me by the
wayside

I will not turn back to pick

    my tarnished pieces up

APATHETIC ABSOLUTION

Confess your crimson sin

Seek penance on bended knee

You plead to beg last rights

Yet your offering is putrid

It curdles and reeks

It is merely an offering

A gutless resolution

A sacrament of sort

I offer you nothing more than

Apathetic absolution

SWIMMING WORDS

Lying here I think of you

Your words doing backstroke in my head

I somehow knew you wouldn't go through

With the things that you had said

That, my dear, makes you the hypocrite

I'm really not that blind

If you think I'll sit and weep and wait

You, my dear,

Have completely lost your mind

MEDIOCRITY

You think she'll give up her freedom for mediocrity?

She thrives on art,

trees,

music

soul

Don't believe she'll settle for anything less

than

magnificent

FROZEN BLOOD

Beat that frozen blood

Oh, blacked hardened heart

I'll even care to lay a wager

That

even angel's tears

    Could not

       cleanse

          your stone-cold soul

IRONY

Eyes fill

With tears of irony

As I stare at vast

Empty forests

While they try

To pave our walkways

    What have we done to deserve the

Respect of mother earth?

Stop hiding behind the big machinery of great

Destruction…..

CROOKED SMILE:
A collaboration with my dear friend, Thomas Hinds – Hindsight Musings

I never expect anyone to look beyond my crooked smile

To see the battles that rage beneath this skin

Behind these eyes of everchanging green there are the deepest bruises and hideous scars I would rather not expose

I am a man built on vicious love and weathered bones

There are teeth marks on this soul. from times I barely made it out alive. Yet this ragged heart steps forward and

continuously saves the day

The war that rages between the heart and mind... one or the other seems to get left behind. like Superman in limbo, I adorn my modern cape as this war rages on but seem to not escape. My bruises have surrendered while colours fade to white. Ragged heart reminder to wave a small white flag. The battle of the rages lay dormant in the mirror. In green eyed reflection, I do see a true soldier, looking straight at me

(Used with permission)

ICE

Don't let the ice in my glass fool you

It really does not match my soul

Don't listen to them, they don't know

but

Only those who care to know,

know this

HOPE HOLDS MY HAND

Standing here
Wishing for a you that doesn't exist
A time will surely come
When hope and a little faith can insist

... but then again

I'm not big of faith....
even if it pretends to hold my hand

FAMILY PHOTOGRAPH

I remember the day we took the family photograph
It's a reminder to me
To live
A year after the photo was taken,
Four family members were taken too

Our story evolved
Changed so much
I'm thankful to know
We were all so happy
Even if for a frozen second

CRINGING SKIN

Cringing skin covered with goosebumps
Teeth gnashing with distaste
Spit those minced up words straight out your aching mouth
Believe each syllable you speak,
unhinge your trestle, so you can scream the things you wish to say

   Please,

      Leave no stone unturned
      No bone unbroken
      No sinew ripped in half
      But do be careful not to choke on
         Unsaid words within your chain bound
            head

LESSONS AND LIGHTBULBS

GRAVEL ON MY KNEE

I tripped and fell on memories and grazed my knee

Ghosts of past swooped over to see the open wound

"Just a flesh wound" they said as tears tried to fill my eyes

        Don't you dare cry, I scorned myself

        it's all but just a scratch,

        up you get and dust it off!

        Look at it! Don't you see?

            All it is, is gravel

            That's stuck across your knee

HEART AND MINDS GREAT QUARREL

Heart and mind were fighting one day,

I'm it!

No! I'm it!

I'm it!

No! I'm it!

This carried on for days, till Soul

had had enough….

Stop your quarrelling at once, for heaven's sake!

It's actually me!

I am the big kahuna here. Without me
neither of you would learn how to work
together

BREATHE AGAIN

One day she said "fuck this" and picked up a pen.
She wrote till her brain could think no more
She ran out of antonyms and synonyms
Forgot to even sometimes breathe
She wrote till all her pens ran dry
She wrote her soul out of tears, so it could no longer cry
She cramped her fingers till her brain had numbed the pain
But still, she wrote
Oh my God, did she write
She bled blue blood from written stone
Abdicated self-doubt off its golden throne
Then, one day she put down the pen and realised
She had no need to write anymore
Her blood, her body, her soul was dry
She had no more need to cry
Her strength regained in fingers red
Her blood stopped running on the page
Her brain remembered words and more
She even got to breathe again

BUTTERFLY WORDS

Butterfly wings

and words

have a lot

in common

The ripple effect

either can cause

could be reason

for tears or applause

SHE'S SCARY

If she scares

the hell out

of you

chances are

she'll bring

out

your

heaven

SEE THE LIGHT

He touched me with his

dark side

Now I really

don't want to see

the light

ELIXER

The elixir of

Life

Death

Love

Hate

Lay in the sounds

That come out of your mouth

RUSTIC RUM AND TAINTED CIGARETTES

She used to drown her sorrows in rustic rum and tainted cigarettes

But she drove herself to the precipice to look down

Into the valley

The valley seemed far enough to engulf and envelop her

burdened, heavy soul

Set free from mortality she climbed the mountain high

Raging rum and sickening cigarettes

Blocked her sense of sensibility

Till all she found was ashes

And an empty glass with ice

REFLECTION

I used to look away

But,

my reflection

insisted

on talking to me

she said hello and I had

to look at her,

she'd been looking for me,

for a damn long time

DARKEST BEFORE DAWN

Apparently, it's supposed to be
darkest before the dawn,
      I disagree.
      It's darkest when
you realise the only thing
      left to do is
          fight

MEASURE OF A MAN

The measure of a man
is how
he looks and talks
to a woman
The measure of a woman
is the
same

BLUE

Blue is the colour of wanderlust
That's showing in her eyes
It will then come as no surprise
When I tell you
That blue is her favourite colour

BREATHE LIFE

Breathe sweet breath of life
Arise to those that fear the living,
Those on the edge of self design
Leaning against the precipice in hopes
of Divine intervention
Take heed, oh weary heart, no need to wait,
Hesitate
Procrastinate
The breath of life fills cracked lungs like
Shutters at the window
Arise, for you have been knighted
Master of your own destiny
Arise! Arise!
Breathe sweet breath of life
And do not fear the living

BARE MY SOUL

I'm not here for loss of love
I've loved, I've lost, I've moved on
I'm not here for loving
I'm not in love and I'm happy with that
My soul is at peace with its own company
I'm here to bleed in letters, words, sentences
I'm here to try say the things
My mouth hesitates to say
I'm here, like you, to bare my soul outright

MEMORIES OF MUSIC

I lie here listening to Eddie Vedder
Memories of music flood my eyes
Musical teardrops seep slowly down
I love that I was taught to love music
Music, birth, death
Three things that are certain
I love that music is the healer, the soother
It's holding my heart with gentle hands
I love that it's lining the crevices of my soul
With healing balm

HOCUS POCUS

Hocus pocus refocus

Till green leaves turn to burnt sienna

And snow from cottonwoods float down to the ground

I swear I hear every sound

Of the creaking, timeless trees

Along riverbanks where they stand proud

And seas that rolled on by,

As you watched the leafless tree stand tall

In the background of a darkening looming storm

I also swear I heard you say my name

In a prim and proper way

SUPPRESSED EMOTIONS

Suppressed emotions become inescapable nightmares
As self-inflicted guilt seeps through your skin
Telling you lies
Of the things you
could have
… would have
… should have done
But then forgiveness comes, in small and deliberate steps
Without the nightmare, you wouldn't awake and forgive
For sweet blissful memory sake

THE RAVEN AND THE BUTTERFLY

The raven eyed the butterfly as she perched with tiny feet
    Then the raven spoke in gentle tones

    "do you know the phoenix?" he quizzed his tiny friend
    "did you know the three of us are symbols of great change?"

        Slowly little butterfly smiled her sweetest smile
  "why yes indeed," she said "you're two birds that flock together
      and I get to grow from
    a caterpillar"

THE UNASSUMING

I love the unassuming
When gifts arise from deep within
Moments when hearts are filled with joy
Tiny lady sings sweet Amazing Grace
surprise and smiles appear on every face

A simple man in stature
leaves eyes and ears in awe
Those are the moments I delight in
So I guess I'm laying down a golden simple rule
the game of pure assumption
is only played by fools

500 THREAD COUNT

I dreamt my dreams on Egyptian cotton linen
The 500-thread count
made it difficult
to iron them out

THE NATURE OF THE BEAUTIFUL BEAST

I think about poetry like a blood thirsty maniac
Feel it
Think it
Write it
Read it
Sight it
Embrace the nature of this
Beautiful tamed beast
The thirst is briefly quenched until….
Feel it
Think it
Write it
Still

I REMEMBER IT

I remember it
I remember feeling disparaging despair
Feeling completely and utterly numb
I remember the noises, sounds, screams, cries in my head
While my mouth felt like a mute
I remember feeling out my body, yet firmly in it still
I remember time zooming past or standing still
I remember statue like behaviour, not knowing what to do
Then, I remembered
It's ok to not be ok
It's ok to ask for help through numb and sobbing tears
I remember knowing it will be ok
It was ok
I remember
I am thankful I made it out of the darkness
Alive. Free from all the noise.
Aware of who I was.
I remembered who I was

FREE FROM ME

I set myself free from me
And only then
Was I truly free
Free to finally see
That truth and beauty flow
From within
But I guess it comes with that
Wisdom
The elderly so often speak of
"get out of your own way"
I finally know now what they
Were trying to say

UNCHANGEABLE THINGS

We only mourn the things
We wish we could change
after
we accept
The things that are
unchangeable

OPEN YOUR PALMS

You only burden yourself
With unnecessary crosses
When you place anothers behaviour
In the control of your hands
Open your palms and set them free
The magical part in all of that
Is you too will set yourself free

HEALING IN THE MAKING

Darkened night
Teary eyes
Favorite music filled with smiles
A special song
Listened twice
Lapping waves
Sweetened grief
Photos captured bittersweet
Heart adjusting to life as is
Heated blanket wrapped a hug
While healing in the making

JEALOUSY AND COURAGE

She said
"Jealousy and courage are opposites,
if you choose jealousy
above courage, walk away
right now"

MOUNTAINS

Mountains are
only small
by distance
Don't get so close
to your mountain
That you cannot enjoy the view.
Step back and see
Your mountain is part
Of a much bigger scene

WORN OUT COURAGE

With worn out courage she raised her voice
To match her clenching fist
"I am more stubborn than you will ever be!"
She shouted to her darkness

MOONLIGHT

        I sometimes sleep
            with my light on
          so the moonlight
      that shines
            in my window
      has company
        and
            therefore
won't keep me awake

OPEN HEARTS

Open hearts
can spit you out,
but, if there is a wall
you always have a place
to hide behind

LEGO BLOCK

You can't break it to build it again
it's not a lego block
you might think it will
but it is very resilient
you tend to underestimate it
the lego block is lead

APATHETIC SILENCES

The apathetic silences
echoed like
a ducks quack in a tin

BLOOD WORDS

My skin is thicker than
the blood words
dripping from your mouth

WORDS OF SWEETNESS

don't just feed me words of sweetness
life isn't all swirly whirly moon
glitter shooting twinkly stars
Sometimes there is no moon
and the darkness devours the night
feed me the darkened words
that float within your mind

Did you not know that we get cavities
from having too much sweet?

BLADELESS SWORD

The bladeless sword called the tongue
can cause the exact same damage as
a sharpened sword

VULNERABLE

I used to hate being vulnerable
I thought it showed weakness
I now know I was very wrong
all it shows is strength

NO FOCUS

thoughts running everywhere
no focus
no tunnel vision
no lookie here
the morning shines in my window
the grey of raining clouds looms outside
I lay patiently for words to make sense in my head
and then it dawns on me
(no pun intended)
just write and see what will be
so here I am
lying
waiting....
patiently

BLUE SKIES

Blue skies, tell me your secrets
do our souls live there?
I guess some questions
will always have assumptive answers

Green trees, tell me your secrets
do our souls live there?
I guess I like that answer best
souls swinging in the breeze
growing, rising up
with tales of history

You say you don't know me.....

I ask,

"Don't you read?"

www.ingramcontent.com/pod-product-compliance
Lightning Source LLC
Chambersburg PA
CBHW040740020526
44107CB00084B/2829